So Many Bikes!
A Kid's Guide To Delft, Netherlands

Photography by John D. Weigand
Poetry by Penelope Dyan

Bellissima Publishing, LLC
Jamul, California
www.bellissimapublishing.com

Copyright © 2015 by Penny D. Weigand and John D. Weigand

All rights reserved. No part of this book may be reproduced or transmitted in any form or by any means, electronic or mechanical, including photocopying, recording, or by any other means, or by any information or storage retrieval system, without permission from the publisher.

ISBN 978-1-61477-194-4
First Edition

Life is like riding a bicycle.
To keep your balance you must keep moving.

Albert Einstein

So Many Bikes!
Bellissima Publishing, LLC

Introduction

The city of Delft sits between The Hague and Rotterdam in Netherlands's southwest. The name, Delft, comes from the Dutch word for digging; and this makes sense, because there are a lot of canals in Delft, which also seems to be a big highlight of other places in the Netherlands as well. You can see the 13th-century Old Church, the 15th-century New Church, and the Prinsenhof, once home to the great William of Orange, now a museum. Delft has long been a center for fine ceramics, and traditional hand painting methods can still be witnessed at Koninklijke Porceleyne Fles. But this 'learn to read' book is not about any of that! This book is about the feel of this place, and it's about what a kid can see and do and notice, all on his or her own, as they practice reading skills through word recognition, word repetition and rhyme.

Travel with award winning author, attorney and former teacher, Penelope Dyan, and with photographer, John D. Weigand, through the pages of this book, and see some of what they saw and feel some of what they felt about this quaint city. Then watch the free music video that goes with this book on the Bellissimavideo YouTube Channel.

So Many Bikes!
Bellissima Publishing, LLC

So Many Bikes!
A Kid's Guide To Delft, Netherlands

Photography by John D. Weigand
Poetry by Penelope Dyan

You get off of the train in Delft
(in the Netherlands)
and there are bicycles as far
as YOU can see!
You and Mom and Dad ALL think
about how healthy
everyone HERE must be!
You look near, and YOU look far.
It seems hardly ANYONE here,
gets around in a CAR!

You walk awhile,
and you get to a store.
You see old-fashioned brooms
and baskets,
milk buckets and more!

And this store doesn't have
a delivery truck.
But nobody who shops HERE
is out of luck!
Because if YOU want something
delivered from INSIDE,
it will come right to you
on a bicycle ride!

In this shop window
are some wooden shoes,
and chairs where you can sit,
and so you look right up at mom,
and ask, "Can we rest a bit?"

There is a man working
in his bicycle shop.
There are so MANY bikes here,
that he works quite A LOT!
Dad says that the man
MIGHT be working on a flat.
He wonders what
YOU think about THAT!
You say that YOU think
it's kind of funny,
because there are so MANY bikes,
that he must make LOTS of money.
Then dad says, "But alas,
nobody here makes much selling gas!"

And here is a fun thing you can do,
you can get your picture taken
next to a giant wooden shoe!
Delft is also VERY well known
for its porcelain of white and blue.
Mom buys a boy and girl kissing
and says,
"This is for me, NOT for YOU!"
Then she buys a necklace
for a VERY good friend,
because when it comes to shopping,
for MOM there's NO end!

You notice that
if people aren't on bikes
as they travel down the street,
they just simply walk around
on their very OWN two feet!
"But where are all the people?"
you ask.
And then by Mom you're told,
"They are probably ALL inside,
because today it's VERY cold!"

You keep on walking.
You are having fun.
You wonder what else you will see,
before this day is done!

You see the cathedral,
bikes are lined up outside.
The doors are closed,
so you don't go inside.

Then over bright flowers
a golden unicorn seems to leap,
from between two windows
where (you decide)
some Netherlanders sleep.
Your feet are aching now.
Dad says HE'S cold.
Mom looks at Dad and says,
"I think I'm getting old!"
Then you all decide it's probably best,
to go to the hotel and get some rest.

Then you see a glass egg of blue.
You THINK you see ONE,
but there's ACTUALLY two!

Then down the empty street
you, Mom and Dad walk.
You are SO cold and tired,
that you don't EVEN talk!
But there IS one thing
about being THERE;
and that's without all the cars,
there's a lot of FRESH air!
And for THAT reason alone,
YOU decide it's all right,
for so MANY people
to ride on a bike!

"You could save the world, one bicycle at a time."

Penelope Dyan

www.ingramcontent.com/pod-product-compliance
Ingram Content Group UK Ltd.
Pitfield, Milton Keynes, MK11 3LW, UK
UKHW060134240426

12048UKWH00002B/39